GIMME GOD
THE JOURNEY OF YOUR UNFOLDING FAITH

ZONDERVAN

GRAND RAPIDS, MICHIGAN 49530

ZONDERVAN.COM/
AUTHOR**TRACKER**

Youth Specialties

www.youthspecialties.com

Gimme God Leader's Guide: The Journey of Your Unfolding Faith
Copyright © 2004 by Youth Specialties

Youth Specialties products, 300 South Pierce Street, El Cajon, CA 92020, are published by
Zondervan, 5300 Patterson Aveunue SE, Grand Rapids, MI 49530

Library of Congress Cataloging-in-Publication Data

Bundschuh, Rick, 1951-
  Gimme God leader's guide : the journey of your unfolding faith / by
Rick Bundschuh.
    p. cm. -- (Highway visual curriculum)
  ISBN-10: 0-310-25831-6 (softcover)
  ISBN-13: 978-0-310-25831-5 (softcover)
 1. Christian education. 2. Christian education of young people. I.
Title. II. Series.
  BV1471.3B86 2004
  268'.433--dc22

2004008612

Unless otherwise indicated, all Scripture quotations are taken from the Holy Bible: New International Version (North American Edition). Copyright © 1973, 1978, 1984 by International Bible Society. Used by permission of Zondervan.

Some of the anecdotal illustrations in this book are true to life and are included with the permission of the persons involved. All other illustrations are composites of real situations, and any resemblance to people living or dead is coincidental.

All rights reserved. No part of this publication may be reproduced, stored in a retrieval system, or tranmitted in any form or by any means—electronic, mechanical, photocopy, recording, or any other—except for brief quotations in printed reviews, without the prior permission of the publisher.

Web site addresses listed in this book were current at the time of publication. Please contact Youth Specialties via e-mail (YS@YouthSpecialties.com) to report URLs that are no longer operational and replacement URLs if available.

Editorial and art direction by Rick Marschall
Edited by Anita Palmer
Proofread by Linnea Lagerquist
Designed by Proxy
Printed in the United States of America

06 07 08 09 10 • 10 9 8 7 6 5 4

07	Avoiding God	1
25	Slapped	2
45	The Plunge	3
61	The River	4
77	Dueling Agendas	5

HIGHWAY VISUAL CURRICULUM

Volume Three

GIMME GOD

Introduction

Welcome to Youth Specialties and Highway Video.

Unlike many teaching tools, Highway Video does not presume to tell you what message to communicate to your flock. Instead, it is designed to be a flexible tool you can use to work with whatever message, purpose, and age level you have. Everything from announcements and teaching moments to benedictions, this material can be used with every age level—from middle school kids on up—and for just about any group size and church style.

But we don't want to leave you hanging.

In this booklet we've provided ideas for a variety of possible ways you can use each film clip. We've also included a lesson plan or two for you to check out and plug in wherever you feel it's appropriate. The lessons written for middle school students are short and action-filled. Those written for high school groups are longer with less action but more abstract thinking.

Our lesson plans even have downloadable, reproducible talksheets and other activity resources. You can download them for free off this Web site:
**www.YouthSpecialties.com/store/downloads
code word: highway3**

To indicate each possible option for using a particular film clip, we've created a Signpost icon. This symbol designates a new path of teaching or communication for the video segment. With just a glance you'll be able to access a wide expanse of alternatives for using each video clip with your group.

Please feel free to manipulate the video in whatever way works best for your purposes.

For example, you may only want to show a portion of the video. Or you may decide that your group should view the clip more than once, maybe showing it to them a second time after you've explored the subject—just as a reminder.

You may download the video into your computer video editing program and clip the time, add a trailer, insert some Scripture, or use whatever device you have at your disposal that will help you communicate the point of your lesson or message.

Look for **Production Notes** and its icon to get behind-the-scenes comments from the producers.

For a couple of the Signposts we have gone ahead and mapped out lesson plans for youth groups that support a particular teaching idea inspired from the film clip. Remember, the talksheet resources for these lessons are integrated in these texts, but they can be downloaded and customized for your use free of charge at
www.YouthSpecialties.com/store/downloads
code word: highway3

Avoiding God 1

Alternate Routes

General Church Use

Try running this little comedy-with-a-serious-message by some of your home Bible studies groups. You can even use ideas from the Small Group Bible study to get a discussion going. This concept ain't just for kids!

Emergent Ministries

Avoiding God is a wonderful starter for a number of messages. Toss it right up there on the screen and use it as a launch pad for some serious personal introspection.

Small Group

Focus: God loves us so much he pursues us.

Biblical basis: Genesis 3:8-10, Daniel 5:1-29, 1:1-2:9, Matthew 27:3-5, Mark 14:66-72

Stuff you need: *Avoiding God* film clip

Getting Started

When God gets on your trail he is hard to shake. Get a discussion going about some of the images that writers have used to describe this pursuing God. Get the discussion rolling by saying something like this:

Writers commenting about God's tenacious love for people have sometimes made comparisons to him as a bloodhound on the trail of a fleeing suspect or as a cat who, once you feed it, keeps on coming back and back again. Some even use the concept that God is like benevolent acid—you can try to block him out but he eventually eats through everything we throw in his way.

What do you think about these comparisons? Do they ring true? Why or why not? Any other comparisons you can think of for God in this way?

If you have older students or more literary oriented students you may want to hand out copies of *The House of Heaven* by Francis Thompson (here are the first few lines; you can get the rest online) and get a discussion going based on this poem.

The Hound of Heaven

I fled Him, down the nights and down the days;

I fled Him, down the arches of the years;

I fled Him, down the labyrinthine ways

Of my own mind; and in the mist of tears

I hid from Him, and under running laughter.

Up vistaed hopes I sped;

And shot, precipitated,

Adown Titanic glooms of chasmèd fears,

From those strong Feet that followed, followed after.

But with unhurrying chase,

And unperturbèd pace,

Deliberate speed, majestic instancy,

They beat -- and a voice beat

More instant than the Feet --

"All things betray thee, who betrayest Me."

Transition to the video clip by saying something like this:

> **Here is another version of this same idea...only in a comic vein. Let's take a look at *Avoiding God* and consider the messages the filmmakers give to us in this piece.**

Or show the video clip *Avoiding God* and discuss it by asking—

> **What tensions did the pursued character have with God?**
>
> **Did God seem annoying? Is God ever annoying?**
>
> **What do you think about the girl's reaction to how God was treated? What message did that have for you?**
>
> **What does this film suggest that God wants from us?**

Transition to the Bible study by saying something like this:

> **I think we can all agree that God lovingly pursues us, but it's what we do about this pursuit that makes a difference...and people have different responses. Let's crack open the Book and see a few examples.**

Bible Study

Ask a number of students to individually look up the following Bible characters and report back on how they responded to God hounding their conscience.

Adam and Eve, after they ate the forbidden fruit—Genesis 3:8-10

Belshazzar, after partying with goods from God's temple—Daniel 5:1-29

Jonah, after being told to preach to Nineveh—Jonah 1:1-2:9

Judas, after betraying Jesus—Matthew 27:3-5

Peter, after denying Jesus—Mark 14:66-72

Ask—

How did the biblical characters respond when they knew they had done something wrong?

Why do you think that some take so long and run so hard from God?

What is it in the heart of a human being that keeps trying to escape God?

What do you think people are afraid of if they let themselves be swept up by God?

Why would some, such as Judas, even choose death rather than repentance?

How do people today attempt to escape the pursing love of God?

Wrap Up

Ask your students to bow their heads and silently reflect on their lives. Ask them to consider if they are running from God in any way and to take this time of quiet and meditation to stop running and allow God to catch them and bow to his will.

Middle School

Focus: You can't run from God

Biblical basis: Jonah 1:1-3:10

Stuff you need: *Avoiding God* film clip; blindfolds for each student; props such as spray bottles with water, megaphone, electric fans, stinky dried fish, sand, sound effect material, etc.; and plenty of help.

Getting Started

Open your session with the *Avoiding God* film clip. Tell your students something like this:

> Today we are going to take a look at a nutty film clip with a heavy message. Let's watch it and see if you can figure out what the filmmakers are trying to communicate.

Watch the film and then let the kids feedback on what they thought the message of the film was.

Transition to the Bible study by saying something like this:

> This film clip is all about how a loving God pursues us at all times trying to get us to respond to him. There is nowhere we can go or hide where God can't pry

us out and get our attention. Probably nobody in the pages of the Bible demonstrates better than the guy whose life we are going to look at today...well, maybe "look at" isn't the right word. "Sense" may be better, because we are going to do something called The Blindfolded Bible Study.

Bible Study

Do a blindfolded Bible study of Jonah with your kids.

Make sure you have enough blindfolds for your kids, and enough staff and props so that the kids are exposed to all the sensations you want them to experience.

You or one assistant will need to be the reader. Read all the text, but for the words in bold, read through a megaphone or use a loud speaker with the amps cranked up. Naturally you can even get crazier than this...but these ideas and suggestions for timing will get you started!

The Text –
Jonah 1:1-4:3 (The Message)

One day long ago, God's Word came to Jonah, Amittai's son: [2] "Up on your feet and on your way to the big city of Nineveh! Preach to them. They're in a bad way and I can't ignore it any longer."

[3] But Jonah got up and went the other direction to Tarshish, running away from God. He went down to the port of Joppa and found a ship headed for Tarshish. He paid the fare and went on

board, joining those going to Tarshish—as far away from God as he could get.

Have your staff start muttering and yelling like sailors, vendors, etc., while they run around the room poking at your kids saying things like, "Hey buddy, need a ticket to Tarshish? Got 'em on sale, cheap!"

[4] But God sent a huge storm at sea, the waves towering.

Now have your staff run around with spray bottles during this whole next section, spraying water on kids, yelling to each other in between verses. Also get a bunch of fans going to blow wind and spray all around. Crack wood and create other sound effects with stuff on hand, or use a sound-effect CD.

The ship was about to break into pieces. [5] The sailors were terrified. They called out in desperation to their gods. They threw everything they were carrying overboard to lighten the ship. Meanwhile, Jonah had gone down into the hold of the ship to take a nap. He was sound asleep. [6] The captain came to him and said, "What's this? Sleeping! Get up! Pray to your god! Maybe your god will see we're in trouble and rescue us." [7] Then the sailors said to one another, "Let's get to the bottom of this. Let's draw straws to identify the culprit on this ship who's responsible for this disaster." So they drew straws. Jonah got the short straw.

[8] Then they grilled him: "Confess. Why this disaster? What is your work? Where do you come from? What country? What family?"

[9] He told them, "I'm a Hebrew. I worship God, the God of heaven who made sea and land."

[10] At that, the men were frightened, really frightened, and said, "What on earth have you done!" As Jonah talked, the sailors realized that he was running away from God.

[11] They said to him, "What are we going to do with you—to get rid of this storm?" By this time the sea was wild, totally out of control.

[12] Jonah said, "Throw me overboard, into the sea. Then the storm will stop. It's all my fault. I'm the cause of the storm. Get rid of me and you'll get rid of the storm."

[13] But no. The men tried rowing back to shore. They made no headway. The storm only got worse and worse, wild and raging.

[14] Then they prayed to God, "O God Don't let us drown because of this man's life, and don't blame us for his death. You are God. Do what you think is best." [15] They took Jonah and threw him overboard. Immediately the sea was quieted down.

[16] The sailors were impressed, no longer terrified by the sea, but in awe of God. They worshiped God, offered a sacrifice, and made vows.

Now for the real fun. Get some really smelly fish at the fish market or the stinky dried fish that comes in a bag and start sticking it under the noses of your kids while the next section is read.

[17] Then God assigned a huge fish to swallow Jonah. Jonah was in the fish's belly three days and nights.

[2:1] Then Jonah prayed to his God from the belly of the fish. [2] He prayed:

> "In trouble, deep trouble, I prayed to God. He answered me. From the belly of the grave I cried, 'Help!' You heard my cry.
>
> [3] You threw me into ocean's depths, into a watery grave, With ocean waves, ocean breakers crashing over me.
>
> [4] I said, 'I've been thrown away, thrown out, out of your sight. I'll never again lay eyes on your Holy Temple.'
>
> [5] Ocean gripped me by the throat. The ancient Abyss grabbed me and held tight. My head was all tangled in seaweed
>
> [6] at the bottom of the sea where the mountains take root. I was as far down as a body can go, and the gates were slamming shut behind me forever— Yet you pulled me up from that grave alive, O God, my God!
>
> [7] When my life was slipping away, I remembered God, And my prayer got through to you, made it all the way to your Holy Temple.
>
> [8] Those who worship hollow gods, god-frauds, walk away from their only true love.
>
> [9] But I'm worshiping you, God, calling out in thanksgiving! And I'll do what I promised I'd do! Salvation belongs to God!"

Get some sand and toss it on to your kids at this point.

> *[10] Then God spoke to the fish, and it vomited up Jonah on the seashore.*

[3:1] Next, God spoke to Jonah a second time: [2] "Up on your feet and on your way to the big city of Nineveh! Preach to them. They're in a bad way and I can't ignore it any longer."

[3] This time Jonah started off straight for Nineveh, obeying God's orders to the letter.

Nineveh was a big city, very big—it took three days to walk across it. [4] Jonah entered the city, went one day's walk and preached, "In forty days Nineveh will be smashed."

Light a bunch of matches (safely!) and let the sulfur smell get around the room before continuing. Then have your staff start to sob and sniffle while the last paragraphs are being read.

[5] The people of Nineveh listened, and trusted God. They proclaimed a citywide fast and dressed in burlap to show their repentance. Everyone did it—rich and poor, famous and obscure, leaders and followers.

[6] When the message reached the king of Nineveh, he got up off his throne, threw down his royal robes, dressed in burlap, and sat down in the dirt. [7] Then he issued a public proclamation throughout Nineveh, authorized by him and his leaders: "Not one drop of water, not one bite of food for man, woman, or animal, including your herds and flocks! [8] Dress them all, both people and animals, in burlap, and send up a cry for help to God. Everyone must turn around, turn back from an evil life and the violent ways that stain their hands. [9] Who knows? Maybe God will turn around and change his mind about us, quit being angry with us and let us live!"

[10] God saw what they had done, that they had turned away from their evil lives. He did change

his mind about them. What he said he would do to them he didn't do.

Let your kids take off their blindfolds and when they settle down kick around a few questions such as—

Why do you think people avoid or run from God?

Why is it foolish to do this?

Someone once said "God will never make you do anything, he will just make you wish you had." How is this true?

How do people today try to avoid or run from God?

Wrap Up

Briefly point out to your students that God pursues us because he loves us and knows what is best for us. Ask your kids to individually create a short document giving God the "Permission to Pursue" them in whatever way he needs to in order to get their attention.

Close in prayer.

High School

Focus: God wants a relationship with us and trying to avoid him is costly and impossible.

Biblical basis: Genesis 3:8-10, Jonah 1:1-2:9, Matthew 27:3-5, Zechariah 7:4-14, 2 Chronicles 36:11-16

Stuff you need: *Avoiding God* film clip, Viewpoint Talksheet, poster board, colored pencils, felt pens, resource people to share their experiences
(You can download the talksheets from www.YouthSpecialties.com/store/downloads *code word:* highway3, *and print or photocopy for your group)*

Getting Started

Idea #1: Ask your students to fill in the blank on this sentence:

What God wants from us is _____.

After your students have commented, show them the *Avoiding God* film clip and then ask them to give you the answer that the *video clip* would give to that question.

Transition to the clip by saying something like this:

Those are some good answers, now let's check out an unusual film clip that attempts to give an answer to that same question.

Idea #2: Get your students together and show them the *Avoiding God* film clip. Then pass out the Viewpoint Talksheet. Ask your students to watch the film again and, when you pause the recording, to fill in the corresponding section of the talksheet.

Pause the film after these scene changes:

Waking up

Bathtub

Skating on the street

Sharing a meal

Paying God off

Meeting with the girl

Reconciliation on the park bench

Viewpoint Talksheet

Scene 1: Waking Up—Right off the bat a comment is made about the nature of God. What is it? (He is there when we awake and when we sleep)

Scene 2: What does this tell us about the personal nature of God? Will God leave us when we demand him to? Why or why not?

Scene 3: What is it about having God as our friend that many are afraid might make them appear ridiculous?

Scene 4: In this scene God seems to be wanting what his "friend" has. What of ours does God ask for?

Scene 5: How do we sometimes try to pay off God so he will "stay out of our way"?

Scene 6: How does God annoy us? At one point the "friend" tells God, "Why don't you just leave me alone?" Is this being honest or mean?

Scene 7: What is it that God wants?

From *Highway Visual Curriculum Book Three – Gimme God*. Permission granted to reproduce this Talksheet only for use in buyer's own youth group. This page can be downloaded from the web site for this book:

www.YouthSpecialties.com/store/downloads code: highway3

Copyright © Youth Specialties.   www.YouthSpecialties.com

After your kids have filled in their responses ask them to share what they have written.

Transition to the Bible study by saying something like this before showing *Avoiding God:*

> **This short film clip brings up all kinds of issues that humans have faced for thousands of years. Let's take a look at how some of those men and women of the Bible became a friend with or avoided God.**

Bible Study

Idea #1: Ask your students to break into pairs or very small groups and come up with a slogan for each type of avoidance that is illustrated by these folks from Scripture.

Adam and Eve, after they ate the forbidden fruit—Genesis 3:8-10

Jonah, after being told to preach to Nineveh—Jonah 1:1-2:9

Judas, after betraying Jesus—Matthew 27:3-5

The people of Israel—Zechariah 7:4-14

Zedekiah—2 Chronicles 36:11-16

Discuss how people avoid God in everyday life. Ask—

What are ways that people try to avoid having God involved in their lives?

Why do people want God to leave them alone?

What are some ways that God seems to show up even to those who don't want him around? What reaction can this get?

Idea #2: Gather the guests you've lined up in advance, or video tapes of several guests if that works best. These are people who at some point in their lives tried to avoid God or drifted from him. They need to be willing to share their experiences, the process of running from God and of returning to him, and to answer any questions your students might have.

Briefly review some of the biblical examples of people who have avoided God. For example—

Adam and Eve, after they ate the forbidden fruit—Genesis 3:8-10

Jonah, after being told to preach to Nineveh—Jonah 1:1-2:9

Judas, after betraying Jesus—Matthew 27:3-5

The people of Israel—Zechariah 7:4-14

Zedekiah—2 Chronicles 36:11-16

Then introduce your guests and allow them to share from firsthand experience the problems, frustrations, and difficulties that can take place when we are trying to keep God at a distance.

Wrap Up

Idea #1: If, as the film clip suggests, what God really wants to do is to hang out with us, how would that happen?

Ask your students to brainstorm a list of suggestions for a person who wants to hang out with God more. These might include turning off distractions and thinking about him, kicking in a worship CD and focusing on the words, spending time in prayer or meditation, reading the Word, and so on.

Close in prayer.

Idea #2: Pass out 5x7-inch sized poster board, colored pencils, felt pens, etc., and ask your student to make a small reminder to hang out with God they can post where they can see it each day. It might say something like "Hang Time?" or "Got a few moments to talk?" — anything that would prompt and remind them to not be too busy or self-absorbed for God.

Encourage students not to just take their poster home but to use them to stay close to God.

Close in prayer.

Production Notes

Avoiding God

Javad Shadzi, Producer

"Gimme God!" It doesn't get any simpler than that. The theme of this volume, *Gimme God,* is particularly close to my heart. One of the most powerful moments in my walk with God was when I realized that God wasn't someone pestering me to live an undesirable life, but that he was the only hope I had to ever be fulfilled in life. I began to see God differently, I began to desire him because I wanted hope and he was my source!

When we were brainstorming ideas for the topic "Avoiding God's Call" we kept stripping down further and further what "God's call" really is so that it could be applied to all people across the board. We kept narrowing it down more and more until what we were left with was simply—hanging out with God. All God wants from us is to be with us. After all, Jesus died so that we could be with God!

But, alas, what does "being with God" really look like, and what if God was really with you one day, sitting at the foot of your bed, following you into the shower, and making your smooth pickup moves look awkward—what would you do, if you accepted that God was really with you?

Bottom line: God is with you always. I'm not positive if he has a British accent but I know he likes ice cream and being a part of your life. Now if he could only make you smoother with the ladies…

Slapped   2

Alternate Routes

General Church Use

With a little help from an editing machine this piece can be shortened in length to make a hilarious e-mail attachment to publicize any event by merely adding a clever tag line. Here are some suggestions: "You won't have to have someone do this to keep yourself awake at (insert time and place here)"; or "No need to punish yourself for missing our sign-up deadline! There is still time, call right away...."etc.

Emergent Ministries

This video, especially edited down a bit, could be a fun, quick way to demonstrate what some people think you need to do to qualify for heaven in God's eyes: punish yourself!

Small Group

Focus: *Slapped* is a bit like a piece of abstract art, kids all think it is funny but often draw different conclusions as to the meaning of the piece. With this in mind, the focus of this small group discussion is a tricky one; how God mysteriously uses the same thing to communicate unique messages to each of us.

Biblical basis: John 12:28-30, Matthew 13:3-1, Luke 10:25-37

Stuff you need: *Slapped* video

Getting Started

Tell your students that they are going to watch a short video clip that needs a moral to it and that you would like them to come up with an idea of what biblical truth they think this short comedy represents. Everyone must play! "I dunno" is not allowed as an answer—you must come up with something!

Show the film clip and after a few minutes to process, involve your kids in a discussion about what *their* interpretation as to the meaning of the film was to them.

Transition to the Bible study by saying something like this:

> **When we come to God's Word, it's interesting how God can show us different things from one teaching or passage of Scripture…and it is very possible that all of those things, those applications of the truth we find in God's Word, can be true at the same time. Let's take a look at a couple of examples…and by the way, I will tell you at the end of the session what idea the filmmakers had in mind when they came up with this script.**

Bible Study

Read Matthew 13:3-15. Then discuss it by throwing out these thoughts:

> This tells us that Jesus told stories to create spiritual readiness – how does this happen if a story or even a passage of scripture is unclear?

Why do you think we remember stories (either told or as in the case today, visual) better than we do a lecture or sermon?

Next read the parable of the Good Samaritan in Luke 10:25-37. As these questions:

This story has a lot of "teachings" in it – What is the main point of the parable and what are some other things that it teaches or implies?

Even if you had no idea what a "Samaritan" was, explain why this story still works.

Sometimes, for some reasons, we may "get" something that others don't get at all. Use the example from John 12:28-30.

Who heard the "voice"?

What were the varying opinions as to what this voice was?

Who did Jesus say this voice was for?

If the voice was for the crowd, why do you think only some of it recognized it as Divine?

Have you ever read a passage of the Bible and got nothing from it and then at a later time found it spoke to you? If so, why do you think this happens?

Wrap Up

Throw out this thought and then discuss it: What do we need to hear God's voice, and for our eyes to be opened to what he wants to show us? Your students may come up with a list that looks a bit like this:

Get rid of distractions

Make sure we are not disconnected from God by open rebellion to him.

Pray for his insight.

Think and meditate on what he says, look at it from all kinds of angles.

List down what they suggest and add any ideas of your own. Ask your students to prayerfully consider if they are in the right "heart place" to be able to hear and see what God is saying and showing them.

Close in prayer.

Middle School

Focus: Should we allow the world to slap our faith around? How to handle persecution for being a Christian.

Biblical basis: John 15:18-21, 1 Peter 3:15, Acts 18:4, Romans 12:14, Matthew 5:44, 1 Peter 2:12

Stuff you need: Pencil and paper; Bibles; chalkboard, whiteboard, or overhead projector; *Slap Me* Talksheet
(Note: You can download the talksheet from www.YouthSpecialties.com/store/downloads *code word: highway3 and photocopy it to use with your group.)*

Getting Started

Come up with a list of insults that get close and personal (not mean, though). Here are some.

He looked out of the window and got arrested for mooning.

You have such a striking face—how many times were you struck?

You have the face of a saint—a Saint Bernard!

When he walks down the street he gets fined for littering.

Everybody has the right to be ugly, but you have abused the privilege.

At a Christmas party, they hung you and kissed the mistletoe!

Do they rub tree branches on your face to make ugly sticks?

When you were a baby, your parents had to feed you with a slingshot.

It looks like she ran the 100-yard dash in a 90-yard gym.

Her picture is on the inside of a Roach Motel.

Her face would make a blind person cry.

You're so stupid, you couldn't find water if you fell down a well.

How can I keep an idiot in suspense? I'll tell you later.

Did you study to be that expertly stupid or does it come naturally?

You are living proof that stupid people should not breed.

When you go to the mind reader, do you get half price?

He's so dumb, even blondes tell jokes about him.

If I've said anything to offend you, I mean it.

I can please only one person per day. Today is not your day. Tomorrow isn't looking good either.

Is your family happy, or do you go home at night?

Your gene pool could use a little chlorine.

Did your parents ever ask you to run away from home?

I bet your mother has a loud bark!

You're a good example of why some animals eat their young.

That was funny! But your mother is funniest—I always find women with beards amusing.

Give each student paper and pencil. Choose how many insults you want to use and ask your students to number a list from one to that number. Then ask them to decide, on a scale of 1-5 (5 being the one that provokes the most response), which insult would get them riled up if someone directed it at them and which would be taken lightly.

Go back and find some of the more stinging insults. Make a transition towards the lesson by telling your students something like this:

> **While a lot of the put downs and insults kids hurl and each other are done in light-hearted fun, once in awhile someone takes deliberate aim and truly tries to hurt and cut with their words. When this happens it is usually a direct assault on an important attribute of that person or on something or someone they value.**

Discuss what it takes for your students to stand up and defend themselves, a friend or family member if they are being put down by others? Ask—

What do you do when someone puts down or slanders someone you know and love?

When, if ever, is it proper to stand up for yourself, a friend or what you believe?

Bible Study

Discuss the fact that for some students, attacking another person's belief in Christ or making fun of Christians, is common. Transition to the video by saying something like this:

As a solution to those put-downs some people quote Matthew 5:39—"But I tell you, do not resist an evil person. If someone strikes you on the right cheek, turn to him the other also." While this may be exactly the right response in some situations it may not be the only possibility. Let's take a look at a short video where the idea of merely taking the "verbal slaps" against our faith is visualized in a hilarious way.

Show the *Slapped* video clip

Ask your kids to kick in their thoughts and feeling about a person who would constantly be slapped around and yet do nothing about it.

What you will no doubt find is that your students see the passiveness illustrated by the subject of the film as a sign of weakness.

Break your students into groups of 2-3 and slide into a study of other biblical responses by saying something like this:

vol chp pg
03: 02: 32

Christians don't have to be weak or passive if someone challenges our faith or tries to paint believers as idiots. We can respond in powerful ways! Let's take a look at a few of them.

On a chalkboard, overhead, whiteboard, or on slips of paper put these references.

1 Peter 3:15 (But in your hearts set apart Christ as Lord. Always be prepared to give an answer to everyone who asks you to give the reason for the hope that you have. But do this with gentleness and respect...)

Acts 18:4 (Every Sabbath he reasoned in the synagogue, trying to persuade Jews and Greeks.)

Romans 12:14 (Bless those who persecute you; bless and do not curse...)

Matthew 5:44 (But I tell you: Love your enemies and pray for those who persecute you...)

1 Peter 2:12 (Live such good lives among the pagans that, though they accuse you of doing wrong, they may see your good deeds and glorify God on the day he visits us...)

Ask each group to look up the passages and to come up with an action list of responses that a Christian could take if they were being hassled by others for their faith. Their lists should look something like this:

Be able to explain our faith in a reasonable way to others.

Be able to be knowledgeable and persuasive in my presentation of my beliefs.

Do a surprise act of kindness for those who hate us and pray for them.

Prove what we believe with the quality of our lives and our actions.

Have your kids share and see how close they get to these ideas. Discuss the fact that some Christians are silent because they know little about their own faith or because the way they live is contrary to the way a Christian ought to live.

Wrap Up

Grab a talksheet you've already customized and pass them out to each student. Tell them something like this:

> **I have a personal message to you from Jesus that can be helpful to remember whenever you are made fun of because you are a believer.**

Slap Me Talksheet

Please insert your name in the blanks from this passage of Scripture (John 15:18-21 The Message):

"If you, _____, find the godless world is hating you, remember it got its start hating me. _____, if you lived on the world's terms, the world would love you as one of its own. But since I picked you, _____, to live on God's terms and no longer on the world's terms, the world is going to hate you.

"When that happens, _____, remember this: Servants don't get better treatment than their masters. If they beat on me, they will certainly beat on you, _____. If they did what I told them, they will do what you tell them.

"They are going to do all these things to you, _____, because of the way they treated me, because they don't know the One who sent me."

From *Highway Visual Curriculum Book Three – Gimme God*. Permission granted to reproduce this Talksheet only for use in buyer's own youth group. This page can be downloaded from the web site for this book:

www.YouthSpecialties.com/store/downloads code: highway3

Copyright © Youth Specialties.   www.YouthSpecialties.com

Close in prayer

High School

Focus: What does God need to do to get you to take some action?

Biblical basis: 1 Samuel 2:22-25, 2:29, 3:11-14, 13:11-14, 15:1-35, 18:1-30, 19:1-24; Exodus 7:14, 7:22-23, 8:15, 8:19, 8:32, 9:7, 9:12, 9:35, 10:20, 10:28; Numbers 14:22, 26-45

Stuff you need: Slapped video; "Whaa Happened?" talksheet. *(Note: You can download the talksheet from* www.YouthSpecialties.com/store/downloads *code word:* highway3 *and photocopy it to use with your group.)*

Getting Started

Idea #1: Ask your students to select how they think they would respond to the following scenario.

"Whaa Happened?" Talksheet

"Whaa Happened?"

Put a check mark next to the statement that says the best how you would react to the following scenario:

You are in a hotel with lots of other kids for a large youth convention. In the middle of the night you hear the fire alarm go off. Would you:

_ Jump right out of bed and run down the stairs wearing only what you were sleeping in.

_ Get up, put on some clothes, make sure you are presentable and then go out.

_ Call someone else in another room or the front desk before leaving the room.

_ Talk to your roommates and decide together what you should do.

_ Panic, cry, write your will, call your mother, etc.

_ Go into the hall to see if you could smell smoke and see what others are doing before doing anything.

_ Figure it is a prank and do nothing until someone knocks on your door.

_ Figure it is a prank and roll over and go back to sleep.

From *Highway Visual Curriculum Book Three – Gimme God*. Permission granted to reproduce this Talksheet only for use in buyer's own youth group. This page can be downloaded from the web site for this book:

www.YouthSpecialties.com/store/downloads code: highway3

Copyright © Youth Specialties. www.YouthSpecialties.com

Discuss the wisdom or foolishness of your group's responses. Transition to the *Slapped* film clip by saying something like this:

> **Regardless of your probable response, we can all agree that the purpose of a fire alarm is to produce action! It is only because people don't take it seriously that they do nothing or stall around when it goes off. While this may or may not be valid when it comes to fire alarms, when it comes to God, he wants to be taken very seriously when he asks for action. Yet, for some people God keeps trying to slap them into action and they do little or nothing. Let's check out a hilarious example of this idea.**

Show the *Slapped* film clip to your students.

Transition to the Bible study by saying something like this:

> **The point of this crazy video is that the guy just stood there and took the slaps without doing anything! This may sound really dumb but people often keep on resisting God even when he is doing everything he can to get them to move! Let's look at some examples.**

Idea #2: Use the *Slapped* clip to kick open a discussion that will lead into the Bible study. Set up the clip by saying something like this:

> **Today I want to show you a short crazy film clip with a serious message behind it. The hands from off screen are God's, the guy in the film is the average Joe. Watch the film and see if you can guess what the film makers are hinting at with this production.**

Slapped

vol chp pg
03: 02: 37

After the film ask your group to toss out their best guesses. Transition to the Bible study by telling them something like this:

> **The filmmakers were suggesting that God does everything he can to get people to move to action, faith or something in life. He will sometimes just keep slapping people in the hope that they will get going. And this has good precedence in Scripture. Let's take a look at some examples.**

Bible Study

Idea #1: Ask your students to break into groups of 3-4. Hand out paper, pencils and assign each group to research at least one of the following adventures in being "slapped" by God. Tell them to report back on what happened, how God kept trying to get their attention and the results.

The Case of the Rowdy Priests and Powerless Parent (1 Samuel 2:22-25, 2:29, 3:11-14)

The King with Heart of Stone and Brain of Mush (Exodus 7:14, 7:22-23, 8:15, 8:19, 8:32, 9:7, 9:12, 9:35, 10:20, 10:28)

The Misadventures of the Faithless Wanderers (Numbers 14:22, 14:26-45)

The King Who Kept Shooting Himself in the Foot! (1 Samuel 13:11-14, 15:1-35, 18:1-30, 19:1-24)

After your students have reported back, jump into a discussion about how and why some people get "slapped" numerous times yet still don't change. Ask questions such as—

- What are some ways that God "slaps" people?
- What does it mean when God uses tough means to wake people up? Is it because God is mad? Vengeful? Loving and caring?
- How are negative consequences to sin a slap up the head to get moving towards God?
- Why do you think some people never get moving even though God keeps working them over?
- Has God ever slapped you? How?
- How does a person know that God is trying to spur them on towards some action?

Sum up the discussion by pointing out that it is God's love for us that tries to get us to move in His direction…by any means possible. Read 2 Chronicles 36:15 (The Message) to your group: "God, the God of their ancestors, repeatedly sent warning messages to them. Out of compassion for both his people and his Temple he wanted to give them every chance possible."

Idea #2: The Slap Your Head Award!

Nowadays they give awards for people who do really stupid things. People who do stupid things that are caught on video can end up on TV. People who kill themselves stupidly can earn the Darwin Award (for ending their gene pool). Perhaps it's time to consider what kind of award should be given (tongue in cheek of course) to those who keep on refusing all the efforts that God brings down to move them in that direction.

If you have a good-humored bunch of kids you can probably get them to come up with such an award and do the research on contenders for it.

Get them started by bringing in a box of weird stuff to fashion an award from. (You can also add gold spray paint, glue etc. if you want to really go wild). Then break your students up into groups of 3-4. Assign each group at least one of the four case studies below to see which they, as a whole, would give the award to.

> The Case of the Rowdy Priests and Powerless Parent (1 Samuel 2:22-25, 2:29, 3:11-14)
>
> The King with Heart of Stone and Brain of Mush (Exodus 7:14, 7:22-23, 8:15, 8:19, 8:32, 9:7, 9:12, 9:35, 10:20, 10:28)
>
> The Misadventures of the Faithless Wanderers (Numbers 14:22, 14:26-45)
>
> The King Who Kept Shooting Himself in the Foot! (1 Samuel 13:11-14, 15:1-35, 18:1-30, 19:1-24)

Tell them that their job is to read up on the case of their particular example of a person or group that God kept trying (unsuccessfully) to whack into submission and to write their name somewhere on the award.

Take a few minutes to move from the past to the present and discuss how God, in his love, sometimes has to get heavy handed even with those who believe in him. Ask—

> **How does God get our attention?**
>
> **How can really bad things be a wake up call to get us to move closer to God?**
>
> **Why do you think some people continue to resist God?**

Obviously God would rather have us respond to him by a whisper than a smack – so how does one hear God whisper or hear him when he speaks softly? What does he use to speak softly to us?

Wrap Up

Idea #1: Ask your crew to consider one thing where God has been asking them to get moving but where they have been stalling. For example, perhaps God has been asking someone to read his word regularly or to break some bad habit. Maybe it is to offer themselves to be a help somewhere, to kick in money to the offering or start the healing process with a person they have been having conflict with. Ask each student to consider that one thing and in prayer, to make it a pledge to God that they will move on it this week.

Idea #2: Someone once said, "God can only steer a moving ship." Perhaps it's time for some of your students to take their Christian life out of the doldrums and into some new adventure. Maybe God has been speaking, prodding or even slapping a few of them to get them moving.

This lesson may be just what your group needs to get to a new level of commitment and obedience. Use this encourage your students to action. Here are some ideas that could be implemented as you wrap up.

> Plan a special meeting to cook up some challenge that kids in the group could adopt—a service project, a discipleship journey, a missions trip, etc.

Create a "Special Forces" group of kids who, with no pressure or one-up-man-ship, commit themselves to a time of spiritual regimentation, prayer, Bible study, serving and faith sharing.

Design accountability partners to help each other keep from becoming the kind of knucklehead that God has to end up trying to slap into submission.

Production Notes

Joe Perez, *Slapped Hand* Actor

There are very few times in life, if any at all, when the Lord Almighty bestows the privilege of slapping your boss in the face. Numerous times. So many times it starts to hurt your hand.

The making of this video was one of those times. Kevin: "Joe! Come on! We need one more person to slap Travis."

I was confused at first. I imagine it sort of like winning the lottery; like being in a haze at first...then the feeling of a schoolgirl at recess overcomes. I dropped everything I was working on and headed to the elevator where the defacing was to commence.

I stared at the record button and knew that at the very push of it—I would be culminating my whole working career here at Highway Video. It was a very intense state of being. My hand cocked, in a fighter's stance, eyes focused on the pores in his cheek, the record button was pushed...Yet my hand fell limp, like a soldier running full bore off the front line...so intent on killing his enemy but mortally wounded...

I guess sometimes I want to believe that something is God's will for me so much that I lose the strength in my hand to bring some serious pain to a face. I know this doesn't make sense now, but it may make sense later. You can't stop the Lord from working.

The Plunge 3

Getting Started

Bring in a variety of magazines and newspapers. Make sure to include tabloids and alternative papers in the mix.

Get a discussion going on the nature of truth, trust, and faith by asking your students to evaluate how much credence they would put in various periodicals such as *Time* magazine, *Rolling Stone, Cosmo, USA Today, The National Enquirer*, etc. Throw out these discussion questions—

Why do you trust one news source over another?

How do you know that the slick, seemingly less sensational news source is really not putting an untruthful spin on their news?

Should newspapers and magazines be required to tell the truth?

How much of what you read do you take on faith and trust? Why?

Transition to the film clip and Bible study by saying something like this:

When you stop and think about it, all of us take a tremendous amount of things on faith every day. We put our faith in doctors (and even not all those who practice medicine are really doctors); we put our faith in weather forecasters, government officials and so on. So putting faith in God is not some random thing that is terribly different from what we do in many other areas. Yet, some people struggle to trust God, especially when he asks us to step out of our comfort zone. Let's take a look at a comic enactment of this same idea.

Bible Study

Play *The Plunge* film clip for your group.

Take a moment to discuss the obvious truths presented in this nutty parable.

The big kid wasn't being asked to do something impossible.

Water was clearly out of the comfort zone of the kid.

The kid had help in the way of the dad and even water wings.

It came down to a choice to trust his father over his fears.

Trust was rewarded with joy.

Take your group on a short tour of parallel stories of doubt and trust from the Scripture. Here are a few to dig up, examine, and discuss.

Daniel 3:1-17—Shadrach and the boys put their faith in God to rescue them.

1 Kings 18:32-38—Elijah takes on the priests of Baal and trusts God to show up.

Matthew 9:20-22—The woman with a tough medical problem who trusted enough in Christ just to touch him with one finger.

Luke 7:1-10—The centurion who trusts the authority of Jesus.

Discuss the nature of doubt and faith by kicking around questions such as—

Is it always wrong to doubt?

Is there such a thing as a reasonable doubt and unreasonable doubt? If so, give some examples.

Where does doubt come from?

How do people get themselves to a place where they can trust?

Should a people commit themselves if they have strong reasonable doubts?

Does a person need to have absolute proof in order to put trust in something? Why or why not?

What is the balance of evidence and trust that God seems to give?

Wrap Up

Ask your students to take a moment and consider if there is one area of their life where they are struggling between faith and doubt. Perhaps they need to take action. Perhaps they need to get more information or understanding to resolve their doubt or even affirm them.

Pass out 3x5 cards and pencils. Ask your students to write down one area where they need to take the plunge of faith and what, if any, action they can do to help them take that final step. This is meant to be a private act, not one to share, so let them know that upfront.

Close in prayer.

Middle School

Focus: The problem of partial commitment

Biblical basis: Luke 9:23-26, Matthew 8:19-22, Mark 12:20, Luke 14:27-33

Stuff you need: Poster board, felt pens, pencil, paper, Bibles

Getting Started

Get things rolling by showing *The Plunge* video to your kids. You don't need to do much of a set up, merely tell your kids that you want to start the session with a film clip of a silly parable that will be used as a base for the topic explored today.

After the film ask your kids if they can figure out the meaning of the parable they have just watched.

As a way to transition to the Bible Study discuss briefly the different ways to enter a pool—

Go in the shallow end step by step.

Slowly slide over the edge.

Be pushed in.

Merely sit on the edge and hold on as you dip different parts of your body into the water.

Note that going off the diving board always means *full commitment*, whereas most of the other entry ways indicate partial or unwilling commitment.

Bible Study

Remind your students that the Christian faith cannot work if done with slight commitment or partial commitment.

Divide your students into groups of 3-4 and ask them to read at least one of the following passages. (Note: you may need to help a middle school kid understand some of these.) Then tell them to come up with a poster that states and illustrates the passage in a way anyone (even someone not familiar with the Bible) can understand.

Luke 9:23-26

Matthew 8:19-22

Mark 12:20

Luke 14:27-33

Have kids share what they have created.

Using getting on an airplane as a metaphor, help your kids see that the nature of Christianity demands taking the plunge of faith. Ask—

Can a person "sort of" be an airplane passenger?

When is a person committed to being on an airplane? When they buy the tickets? Arrive at the airport? Go through check in? Security? The waiting room? The loading ramp? Sitting in the seat?

What kind of faith does it take to get on a plane?

Do you usually see the pilot of the plane before you fly? How is this similar to the Christian walk?

What does the "flight experience" of someone else do for you?

Wrap Up

By the end of this lesson your students will no doubt see that being a Christian involves a complete step of faith, a plunge taken with heart, soul and mind. This might be a great time to invite students to consider whether they have really taken this plunge for themselves or have only dipped themselves into Christianity.

Close by saying a prayer something like this that your kids could repeat silently to themselves:

Lord, I know that you gave yourself completely for me and now I give myself completely to you. I come with no half measures or hesitation. I offer you my heart, my soul, my mind and my whole life to do with as you please. Amen.

High School

Focus: Faith is what it takes to please God

Biblical basis: Biblical basis: Matthew 14:22-33, 1 Kings 18:32-38, Judges 7:1-23, Daniel 3:1-17, John 20:19-24, Hebrews 11:1 and 6, Romans 4:16, John 3:15-16, 1 Peter 8-9, Galatians 2:16

Stuff you need: *My Faith Meter* Talksheet
(Note: You can download the talksheet from www.YouthSpecialties.com/store/downloads *code word:* highway3 *and photocopy it to use with your group.)*
rat traps, $10 bill, paper, pencils, chalkboard, overhead projector

Getting Started

Idea #1: Kick into the session by showing your students *The Plunge* film clip. Then have a short discussion about the nature of doubt, faith, and being foolish, using questions such as—

What is the point of this comic parable?

Most of us can laugh at the idea of a big ol' guy being fearful of jumping off a diving board but how would you react if you were asked to go off a 40-foot diving platform? Would you blame someone for hesitating at that height?

> The Plunge
>
> vol chp pg
> 03: 03: 51

How do you think the plunge of faith is different for each person?

What's the difference between honest doubt, reasonable faith and foolish faith?

Idea #2: Get two rat traps. Set one, the other carefully soldered so that the snap bar is set "open." Make sure to do this so that the solder points can't be seen. This should give your rat trap the appearance of danger but with no real risk (if you do a good job soldering!). Fold up a $10 bill and stick it in the bait holder of the trap.

Open by commenting a bit on the nature of doubt, reasonable faith, and blind faith. Discuss that idea that everyone decides who and what they will put their faith into. Set up for the stunt by pointing out that you consider yourself trust*worthy* (you might want to get a show of hands in agreement or disagreement on this point) and that you can be counted on to have only the good of students at heart.

At this point bring out both rat traps. Demonstrate the destructive power of the first unsoldered trap by snapping the bar with a pencil (it will break the pencil). Point out that while this trap can do a number on someone's pinky, you are confident that the reflex abilities of your students are better than the trap mechanism. To prove the point you have placed $10 in the bait tray for any student who will reach in and grab it with their hands. And by the way, give them your personal assurance that they won't get hurt.

Now your kids have a dilemma. Do they believe what they see or what you tell them? Which do they trust more—their experience with traps or their experience with you?

Hopefully some brave soul will come and snatch the money from the trap...proving that you were worthy of that kid's faith.

(Put the traps away so that the secret dies with you and continue on with the session!)

Transition to the film clip by saying something like this:

> **Faith, doubt, trust, foolishness are all issues that every Christian must struggle with. Let's take a look at a wacky parable that illustrates some of these things.**

Show the film clip and enter into a discussion with questions such as—

> **What is the point of this comic parable?**
>
> **Most of us can laugh at the idea of a big ol' guy being fearful of jumping off a diving board but how would you react if you were asked to go off a 40-foot diving platform? Would you blame someone for hesitating at that height?**
>
> **How do you think the plunge of faith is different for each person?**
>
> **What's the difference between honest doubt, reasonable faith, and foolish faith?**

Bible Study

Idea #1: Divide into groups of 6-8 students. These groups are to be split into two subgroups— the thumbs-up group and thumps-down group, or the doubters group and believer group. Assign each group at least one of the following passages and ask each subgroup to approach the passage from their vantage point—seeing all the reasons to trust or seeing all the reasons not to trust.

Matthew 14:22-33

1 Kings 18:32-38

Judges 7:1-23

Daniel 3:1-17

John 20:19-24

Have your students explore and share their results. Discuss whether God requires us to have blind faith or reasonable faith and how much information and understanding is required to have reasonable faith. Ask your students why they have any sympathy for those who might struggle in the area of faith.

Idea #2: Ask your students to work in pairs to complete a "Top Ten Reasons to Put Your Faith in God" – let them brainstorm freely. These passages will give them some good ideas for things to include in their list: Hebrews 11:1,6; Romans 4:16; John 3:15-16; 1 Peter 8-9; Galatians 2:16.

Have your students share what they have created.

Consider the nature of faith—why it is easy for some, hard for others and yet entirely reasonable when it comes to God by using the example of faith we exercise whenever we get in an airplane. Use these discussion questions to help your students see the similarity in how we put our trust in Christ.

Can a person "sort of" be an airplane pas-

senger?

Can a person be "sort of" a Christian?

When is a person committed to being on an airplane? When they buy the tickets? Arrive at the airport? Go through check in? Security? The waiting room? The loading ramp? Sitting in the seat?

When is a person committed as a Christian? When they come from a believing family? When they attend church? Become a member? Raise their hand?

What kind of faith does it take to get on a plane?

What kind of faith does it take to really be a Christian?

Do people on planes ever experience doubt or fear?

Do Christians ever experience doubt or fear?

Do you usually see the pilot of the plane before you fly? How is this similar to the Christian walk?

What does the "flight experience" of someone else do for you?

What does the sharing of our faith do to help someone else take the step of faith?

My Faith Meter Talksheet

My Faith Meter

Does faith come easy or hard to you? Evaluate yourself by circling the most typical answer for you:

I can trust God even when I don't see the sense of what he wants me to do.

    Low voltage / Got Some Sparks
    Batteries Good / High Voltage

I can trust and obey God easily even if I am all alone in my decision.

    Low voltage / Got Some Sparks
    Batteries Good / High Voltage

I find it pretty easy to trust God even in the middle of difficult or discouraging stuff.

    Low voltage / Got Some Sparks
    Batteries Good / High Voltage

I find faith comes easily to me, I don't need to be convinced or overwhelmed with evidence.

    Low voltage / Got Some Sparks
    Batteries Good / High Voltage

From *Highway Visual Curriculum Book Three – Gimme God*. Permission granted to reproduce this Talksheet only for use in buyer's own youth group. This page can be downloaded from the web site for this book:

www.YouthSpecialties.com/store/downloads code: highway3

Copyright © Youth Specialties. www.YouthSpecialties.com

Wrap Up

Idea #1: Pass out to each student a copy of *My Faith Meter* Talksheet.

Ask them to evaluate how easy or hard it is for them to trust God. Close in prayer asking for the ability and wisdom to trust God more.

Idea #2: Ask your students to help you list on a chalkboard or overhead as many things that are important to them as possible: friends, family, future, boyfriends, girlfriends, school, sports, material things, etc.

Pass out pencils and paper to each student. Ask them to write the following lines and fill in the blank with something from that list that is personal to them:

Dear God,

    I know that even though I can't see you I can trust you. And I know that I can truly trust you with my_____.

    Signed,

    _____

After kids have completed this short declaration of trust, close in prayer.

Production Notes

The Plunge (Afraid to Follow)
Travis Reed, Producer

My son Marty and I have always wanted to work together, but our schedules had never worked out. So when, through some strange circumstances that I won't bore you with, Marty and I were able to audition for the two roles, we jumped at the opportunity. We never told the producers we were a father-son team until after the audition. They flipped out. Seriously, they couldn't believe it. For the record, we wanted to get the parts based on talent, not because of Me and Marty's "biological connection."

The production on *The Plunge* started right away, which caught Marty and me off guard, since we hadn't been able, due to our schedules and some strange circumstances that I don't want to talk about, to get to the YMCA to work on some "muscle toning." For the record, Marty and I are both passionate about chiseling every muscle to its maximum—as a form of worship, naturally. But again, due to some extraordinary circumstances, Marty and I have been forced to forfeit or passion for regular exercise, initiating the "dismantling of our bodies," which, unfortunately, came across pretty clear in the video. Whoever they hired for wardrobe did a terrible job sizing bathing suits.

Anyway, the shoot went well. The crew on the set could smell the chemistry between Me and Marty. Literally. The only hiccup in the production was the scene where I got attacked by the pool cleaner.

I've never worked with the Barracuda G3 (retails for $299.99) and advanced training wasn't in the budget. Anyway, we were pretty much back to finishing shooting the scene about an hour after the paramedics did their thing. All in all it was a great day. I think the joy of acting with my son really shines through in this piece. People say, "Wow, that scene at the end, with the bubbles...amazing." I tell them, "You know why it was comes off so powerful? Because, we weren't acting."

The River 4

Alternate Routes

General Church Use

This is a beautiful piece to show prior to the start of a worship service. Simply run the video for those who arrive early or who would appreciate a pre-service time of meditation.

Emergent Ministries

Toss in this video clip as a part of a short meditation on letting go of our sins, troubles, and problems, and plunging ourselves into the care of God.

Getting Started

Ask your group to fill in the blank of the following dumb poem with metaphors –

Why I Left Her

> Her hair was smooth as _____,
>
> her eyes flashed like _____,
>
> her lips were as red as _____
>
> and her teeth were as white as _____
>
> but her feet smelled like _____.

Ask your group to define the word *simile* or *metaphor* (figure of speech, imagery) and then ask if anyone knows how the word *river* is used in the Bible as a metaphor. After your group has ventured their guesses tell them that the word is often used to symbolize *salvation*.

Transition to the Bible study by saying something like this:

Let's consider a few images that the word *river* provides that have links with a person's salvation.

Bible Study

Discuss what it is about a river that has spiritual connotations. Use questions such as—

What did a river provide for ancient people? (Refreshment, food, personal cleansing, removal of pollutants, transportation, or even escape from danger.)

Can you think of any songs, hymns or spirituals that use the idea of a river as a metaphor?

Pass out paper and pencils and ask your students to look up the following passages: Psalm 36:8; Psalm 46:4; Isaiah 32:2; Ezekiel 47:1-12; and Revelations 22:1-2. Prompt them with this—

See if you can describe what is implied or meant by the different uses of the word river in these passages.

Ask them to jot their ideas on paper for use in later discussion. Meanwhile, have them report back on what they have discovered. Discuss questions such as—

What are some of the meanings behind the images used in these various scriptures?

What do those words tell us about who God is and what he does for us?

How might tying an attribute of God to a physical creation (such as a river) be helpful to human beings?

Which description of God or His care do you find most compelling?

Wrap Up

Use the film clip *The River* to wrap up your session. Transition to the film by saying something like this:

The idea that God cleanses and takes away the burdens the same way that a river does is a popular image that has encouraged people all through history. Let's take a minute and experience another visualization of that same theme in this film clip. As you watch, see if these images touch your experience in coming to Christ and allowing His living water to wash away your burdens and sins.

Close in prayer after the video.

 Middle School

Focus: A river symbolizes forgiveness of sin in our lives

Biblical basis: Psalm 36:8, 46:4

Stuff you need: Film clip of *The River*, felt pens, vehicles and drivers to get all your students to the bank of a river (you may need to do some advance publicity to make sure your students wear the appropriate attire for an on-site activity) ... if possible!

Getting Started

Launch this Bible study by showing the video clip *The River* to your students. Set up the film by saying something like this:

I would like you to take a look at this short video clip which uses symbolism for an important idea in our Christian faith. See if you can figure out the symbols and what they might stand for.

After the film briefly discuss some of the symbols, such as the baggage, the water, taking the plunge, etc. See if your kids can even get near any of them. Then load them up into the car and head for the nearest river.

Bible Study

Go on-site to teach your students with a living object lesson.

On the bank of the river read and talk about these passages from Psalms.

Psalm 36:8 — "They feast on the abundance of your house; you give them drink from your river of delights."

Psalm 46:4 — "There is a river whose streams make glad the city of God, the holy place where the Most High dwells."

Discuss with your students why a river is sometimes used in the Bible to refer to God's abundance and salvation. A river provides life, sustenance, cleansing, safety, beauty, and so on.

Describe how in ancient days people would use water in ways to carry off the refuse of the towns that otherwise would pollute them. Parallel that idea with the concept that we cast our sin in the river of God's forgiveness and it is carried off forever.

Wrap Up

Ask your students to find a flat stick, a chunk of wood, a large leaf, or something similar. Hand out felt pens and have them write down a word that stands for something they did this week that was contrary to what God would have wanted them to do. (One word will do, they don't need to write out the whole story.) Invite them to ask God's forgiveness for that sin and then to cast it into the river to be taken away forever.

Close in prayer

High School

Focus: God gives us a picture of his love for us and work in us.

Biblical basis: 2 Samuel 22:32, 47; 2 Samuel 23:3; Psalm 17:8, 18:2, 31:2, 36:8, 40:2, 46:4, 61:4, 63:7, 91:4; Proverbs 20:15; Isaiah 17:10, 32:2; Ezekiel 47:1-12; Matthew 16:18, 23:37; John 3:8, 4:14, 7:37-39; 1 Corinthians 10:4; Revelations 21:6; 21:19-20, 22:1-2, 22:17

Stuff you need: Film clip of *The River*, paper, pencils, bars of soap, art supplies, video camera, computers, guitars, "*He Is Like…*" Talksheet
(Note: You can download the talksheets from www.YouthSpecialties.com/store/downloads code: highway3 and print or photocopy for your group)

Getting Started

Idea #1: Ask your kids to help you with a contest. There is a winner for guys and girls.

Invite all of your students to stand. Ask those who have gone without a bath for more than three days to stay standing. Move along to four days, five days, etc. The last girl to sit down and the last guy to sit down win! (Don't forget to ask the circumstances that led to this odorous occasion.) The prize for each is a bar of soap.

Use this stunt to talk about how good it feels to get the grime off of you after getting filthy, sweaty or dirty merely cruising around in the world.

Transition to the Bible Study by saying something like this:

> **Today we are going to consider the refreshing nature of God's love, salvation and forgiveness. God often likens the spiritual realm to our physical one to give us a small taste of his pleasures or the beauty or preciousness of part of his creation. Let's consider some of those.**

Idea #2: Pass out paper and pencils to your students. Tell them that you are going to say a word and, just like in a psych test, you want them to write down the first word that pops into their mind ("word association"). For example, if you say the word *spider* perhaps the first word that comes into your head would be *ugly*, or *scary*, or *stomp*, or even *cool*—depending on your experience and relationship with those bugs.

Try out these words: cotton candy, gym socks, teddy bear, snow, some current TV show, Abe Lincoln, Christmas, castle, gum, knucklehead…(Of course you can add any kind of words to this that you like.)

Ask your kids to read back what they have written. Be prepared for some hilarious responses.

Transition to the video by saying something like this:

> While some words produce strange or nutty responses from us, the language of the Bible uses words and images to give us a picture of what God is doing and wants to do. Let's take a minute and watch a film clip that uses images to communicate spiritual ideas.

Show the film and then discuss what images were in the movie and what spiritual ideas were being presented by the filmmakers.

Transition to the Bible study by saying something like this:

> This film gives only a few images of what God is like and what he is doing. Let's take a look in the Bible for some similar descriptions.

Bible Study

Idea #1: If you haven't used the film clip yet, this would be an ideal place to play the video and show your students how one group of artists used images to put across a spiritual idea.

Divide your students into groups of 3-4 and assign each group a passage of Scripture to explore. After they have found the similes or metaphor in their passages, ask them to sum up by giving the *reason* why or how God or his Kingdom is like this metaphor or figure of speech.

ROCK—2 Samuel 22:32; 2 Samuel 22:47; 2 Samuel 23:3; Psalm 18:2; Psalm 31:2; Psalm 40:2; Isaiah 17:10; Isaiah 32:2; Matthew 16:18; 1 Corinthians 10:4

WATER—John 4:14; John 7:37-39; Revelations 21:6; Revelations 22:17

WING—Psalm 17:8, Psalm 61:4, Psalm 63:7, Psalm 91:4, Matthew 23:37

WIND—John 3:8

JEWELS and PRECIOUS STONES—Revelations 21:19-20, Proverbs 20:15

RIVER—Psalm 36:8; Psalm 46:4; Isaiah 32:2; Ezekiel 47:1-12; Revelations 22:1-2

Ask your students to take a moment and individually fill out the "*He Is Like...*" Talksheet by expressing how God is like those attributes to them personally.

"*He Is Like...*" Talksheet

HE IS LIKE...

For me, God is like a Rock because…

For me, God is like Water because…

For Me, God is like the Wing of a Bird because…

For Me, God is like the Wind because…

For Me, God is like Jewels or Precious Stones because…

For Me, God is like a River because…

From *Highway Visual Curriculum Book Three – Gimme God*. Permission granted to reproduce this Talksheet only for use in buyer's own youth group. This page can be downloaded from the web site for this book:

www.YouthSpecialties.com/store/downloads code: highway3

Copyright © Youth Specialties.   www.YouthSpecialties.com

Ask your students to share from their vantage point why God is like those things to them.

Idea #2: This idea may take some extra time outside of your meeting hour but the results could be a really cool addition to your youth group.

You will need to make sure to have the materials and gear at hand for students to get to work on; art supplies, video camera, computers, guitars, etc.

Divide your group by those who have an interest in the following subjects:

- Drawing/ Design
- Video Production
- Music
- Dance/Drama
- Writing/ Poetry

Tell your group that you would like them to explore the following passages and using at least one of the metaphors for God come up with a t-shirt design or visual image, short video piece, song of worship, drama or dance presentation, a written motto or poem or some other work of art that can be replicated or enjoyed by others.

If you haven't used the film clip yet, this would be a great place to utilize it as a demonstration of how one group of artists visualized a spiritual concept.

> ROCK—2 Samuel 22:32; 2 Samuel 22:47; 2 Samuel 23:3; Psalm 18:2; Psalm 31:2; Psalm 40:2; Isaiah 17:10; Isaiah 32:2; Matthew 16:18; 1 Corinthians 10:4
>
> WATER—John 4:14; John 7:37-39; Revelations 21:6; Revelations 22:17
>
> WING—Psalm 17:8, Psalm 61:4, Psalm 63:7, Psalm 91:4, Matthew 23:37
>
> WIND—John 3:8
>
> JEWELS and PRECIOUS STONES— Revelations 21:19-20, Proverbs 20:15
>
> RIVER—Psalm 36:8; Psalm 46:4; Isaiah 32:2; Ezekiel 47:1-12; Revelations 22:1-2

Naturally, not all of your students may develop their ideas to the fullest, but enough kids may to be able to produce something very powerful to be used for the youth group or church as a whole. Encourage that any designs or productions that are particularly good to be taken to completion.

Have students be prepared to share what they have come up with towards the end of your time.

Wrap Up

Idea #1: Locate a modern worship song that uses metaphors to worship God. Review the words of the song and then sing it together as a moment of praise.

Idea #2: As a closing meditation ask your students read John 5:1-9 and then take a look at the words to this old African-American spiritual which was often sung by slaves. See if they can see how the metaphors used gave them hope and promise.

Ask questions such as—

What is the hope this old song is talking about?

Why would this song be a powerful one among people who were slaves?

What is the spiritual meaning of the images in this song? Note: some spirituals had dual meanings and even codes imbedded in them to help runaway slaves avoid capture.

If you can find a copy of the song you may wish to play it for your group or simply have them read the words from the "*Wade in the Water*" Talksheet as a prayer from their own heart.

"*Wade In the Water*"

"Wade in the Water"

  Chorus: Wade in the water

  Wade in the water, children

  Wade in the water

  Don't you know that

  God's gonna trouble the water;

  Don't you know that

  God's gonna trouble the water.

  I stepped in water and the water is cold.

  Don't you know that

  God's gonna trouble the water.

Said it chilled my body but not my soul.
Don't you know that
God's gonna trouble the water.

Chorus

Well I went to the water one day to pray.
Don't you know that
God's gonna trouble the water.
And my soul got happy and I stayed all day.

Don't you know that
God's gonna trouble the water

Chorus

There is love, In the water,
There is joy, In your water,
Your peace Is in the water,
Your deliverance is in the water.
Oh step in, step in,
Joy is in the water, In the water.
Oh step in, step in.

Love is in the water.
Oh step in, For deliverance
Everything is In the water,
Everything you need.
God's gonna trouble the water.
God's gonna trouble the water.

From *Highway Visual Curriculum Book Three – Gimme God*. Permission granted to reproduce this Talksheet only for use in buyer's own youth group. This page can be downloaded from the web site for this book:

www.YouthSpecialties.com/store/downloads code: highway3

Copyright © Youth Specialties. www.YouthSpecialties.com

Production Notes

The River (Genuine Desire)

Travis Reed, Director

I was cruising down a stretch of California's historic El Camino Real…FYI, at the same time that the American colonies were rebelling against England, a handful of Spaniards and Mexicans established outposts up the California coast. The first was established in 1769 at San Diego, where they established a fortress and a Franciscan mission. From that point, a series of small self-reliant religious missions were established. Each was a day's travel apart and linked by El Camino Real ("The King's Highway"). Overall, El Camino Real linked 21 missions, pueblos and four presidios from San Diego to Sonoma and…

What was I talking about? What was I talking about? Leotards and flags? No? Oh yeah, sorry, *The River* video. Cool. Yeah I was cruising in my '87 Mercedes 4-door, bullet-proof, mafia boat, blasting the tune "The River," by the Chris Tomlin Band, on the six-speaker, "heavy-ampage-induced" Alpine, when the idea for the video pierced my bald skull.

The song just broke me: "When I was held up in chains, The River was free, When I was covered in stains, The River was clean, When I was losing my way, The River found me." The lyrics captured the story of my life. I was dragging a load of soul-wrenching, love-crippling chains around attempting to manufacture "the joy of life" on my own. For me The River, Christ, washed the chains away. The tune continues on: "When we were broken inside, *The River* was love, When we were thirsty and dry, You were more than enough, When we were drowning in lies, The River saved us." Oh man, it gets me every time. Dude, I was drowning. I was drowning in a lot of the ways we drown when we seek fulfillment in the world, but for me my deepest thirst was to be known, to genuinely be loved and to genuinely love. I was broken and the River of Life saved me.

As I reflected on my life and the song and tried to disguise my tears from my fellow El Camino travelers, I thought about my best friend from college, Miles Daisher. He's this crazy, freak-o-nature, extreme sports guy. (Check out his show *Extreme Tribes* on the Discovery channel or do a web search for Miles Daisher and you'll see what I mean). Anyway, as I cruised, the entire video ran in my head shot for shot. I thought, how cool would it be to film my buddy, who hasn't yet met his Creator, to be the guy in the video to launch off the cliff into "The River of New Life." The first time Miles heard the song, he asked what it was about, and we explained the meaning of the song and the "story" behind the video.

He listened. He isn't truly free; he doesn't genuinely know his Creator. Yet.

Dueling Agendas   5

A WILDCARD FILM CLIP

Dueling Agendas is a hilarious wildcard video clip that steals images from a mercifully long-forgotten and short-lived TV spy/ kung-fu/ action/ show of the '70s and adds a goofball audio track complete with dialogue that doesn't match the lips as silly sound effects.

Your kids will at first be baffled and then within seconds be roaring in laughter.

If you try *real* hard you might be able to find some kind of spiritual lesson buried in this nutty film clip…but we don't recommend you try. Just enjoy the ride. OR try a free-association session and have the kids – when they catch their breath – throw out some biblical principles that were ball-parked, or skirted, in the clip. Some surprising ideas might develop.

Here a few ideas on how you can start this with your group.

OPENER

Use *Dueling Agendas* to grab your students' attention and get their bottoms planted in a seat. A video like this says, "We are going to have fun!" so make sure to follow it with something that is high energy.

Don't forget that this clip might be a perfect way to kick off a camp or retreat or any other event where to start with a bit of goofiness is what is needed.

COMIC RELIEF

Sometimes there is a need for a little comic relief. Perhaps your kids have been in serious seminars at a retreat all morning and you are looking for something to relax them up and balance them out. Just grab *Dueling Agendas*. It will do the trick.

'70s PARTY

Throwing a disco? Doing a '70s party for Halloween? Well here you go, now you have perfect addition to your party.

OR...

At the "end of the day" – and when all otherwise logical themes seem dried up, review the "action" and the "story" of the video nonsense. Then ask the kids if, after all, when God looks at our own actions – trying to please him as we go about our lives, or interacting with others – can we see that our own lives must look something like that to God? Can this inspire us to act a little more sanely... to remember to think how our actions look in God's eyes?

Production Notes

Dueling Agendas

Kevin Marks, screenwriter

Travis ordered a handful of films online that are now public domain. The masterpiece you see here is *Black Samurai*, released in 1976. We decided to do a voiceover comedy about this secret agent (Stephen Brockenschmiel) who's hired to retrieve "The Thing" for the U.S. government. I think the lunacy of this piece reflects what it's often like when you've got a different agenda from someone, and you're constantly butting heads with them (or in this case, busting them up kung-fu style and grabbing them in the groin). We often forget what it is we're arguing about, just as we have no idea what "The Thing" is in this video.

My favorite part is when Stephen nearly beats up a tree. He's so charged up after leaving a fight scene that he looks at the tree and says, "You want some?" I admit, there have been times in my life when I've been so angry I've felt like beating up trees or other helpless shrubbery. It's times like those when I need to just put on a fresh sweatsuit, strap on the jet pack, and get out of town for a few days.